BRIDGE

FOR PEOPLE WHO DON'T KNOW
ONE CARD FROM ANOTHER

BRIDGE

FOR PEOPLE WHO DON'T KNOW
ONE CARD FROM ANOTHER

Ray Young

LONDON
W. FOULSHAM & CO. LTD.
NEW YORK - TORONTO - CAPE TOWN - SYDNEY

W. FOULSHAM & CO. LTD.
Yeovil Road, Slough, Berks., England.

LIBRARY OF CONGRESS CATALOGUE CARD NO. 64—15641

572 - 00026 - X

MADE AND PRINTED IN GREAT BRITAIN AT
THE CAMELOT PRESS LTD, SOUTHAMPTON

To Rayme

author's preface

Countless thousands of bright youngsters (and oldsters) deny themselves the pleasures of contract bridge because they think they'll appear "stupid" at their first lesson.

Other countless thousands never get past the first page of even a beginner's bridge book.

Bridge is not that hard once you leap the first hurdles, but the first hurdles can seem imposing indeed to someone who has never played a card game more complicated than "Snap".

The fact that there are 52 cards to keep track of seems like just too much. Complicated further with suits and no-trump, doubles and re-doubles, and a bewildering jargon understandable only to the initiates, and the average beginner needs the courage of a lion to sit down at the bridge table.

This book strips aside most of the mystery that baffles beginners. It explains all the basics that you need to know before you can play—or even read about—the game intelligently.

For best results try to read this book all the way through in one sitting. In thirty minutes or so, you will have a good picture of what the fascinating game of contract bridge is all about. Then go back at your leisure and study each section.

In less time and with less effort than you ever thought possible, you'll be playing bridge—the *best* of the card games.

BRIDGE

**FOR PEOPLE WHO DON'T KNOW
ONE CARD FROM ANOTHER**

one card from another

Bridge is played by four people who sometimes shout at each other but still manage to have lots of fun. Two are partners against the other two.

Partners sit opposite each other. This is a very handy arrangement when they get mad at each other. They can glare and holler and mutter, but the table being between them keeps them from hitting each other easily.

The game is played with two packs of cards. Only one pack is used at a time, however. There are 52 cards in each pack after you throw out the "Joker" cards that come with each new pack.

Before you start the game, take one pack and "cut" for deal. The player who picks or cuts the highest card becomes the dealer.

All 52 cards are dealt out face down one at a time from left to right. The first one to get a card is the player to the left of the dealer. The last one to get a card is the dealer, and if he has done his job right without being fumble-fingered, each person will have 13 cards. These 13 cards make up your "hand".

Unless you have the memory, cunning, and expert card sense of a river boat gambler, you will want to sort your 13 cards into suit and into some kind of order.

This sorting isn't hard to do at all. The pack contains four **suits** of 13 cards each: ♠ spades, ♡ hearts, ◇ diamonds, and ♣ clubs. Put all your cards in each suit together.

Now put all your cards in each suit together according to which one is more important. This is only a little harder to do.

All you have to remember is that the ace of a suit is the top dog, the king comes next, then the queen, then the jack, and then the ten, nine, eight, etc., down to the two or "deuce". In other words, the ace of a suit has top **rank**. Then the king has next rank, then the queen, then the jack, etc.

Now, one more thing to remember about suits and ranks.

The most important suit—the one that has the highest rank—is **spades**. The word spades comes from the Spanish word **espadas**, meaning swords, which only noblemen toted. As you will learn later, spades can be a very noble suit indeed.

The next most important suit is **hearts**. This suit got its name from the English translation of the thoroughly unpronounceable French words *gens de choeur* or choir men. You'll find later that you can make beautiful music with cards of this suit . . . if you have enough of them.

The next most important suit is **diamonds**. And this suit got its name not from diamonds but from tiles. Tiles represented the merchants of old who sold all kinds of this—not necessarily diamonds. Somebody, way back when, tilted a tile on its side and decided it looked very much like a diamond.

The least important, lowest ranking suit of all is **clubs**. How this suit got its name is a mystery. The symbol for clubs is really a clover leaf, and it stood for the peasants who grew all kinds of things—not necessarily clover.

Now that you know how the cards and suits rank, let's see how to use this information to win tricks.

A **trick** is made up of four cards (one from each hand at the table), and the whole object of the game is to win or "take" tricks. You can do this two ways: at no-trump (where just the high cards win) or at a trump contract (where even low cards can win *if* they are in the trump suit and *if* you don't have any cards in the suit led).

Let's look at a couple of sample tricks:

At no-trump, you win this trick because you have the highest card (the jack).

♠ 3

PLAYER A   ♠ *Ace*   ♠ 5   PLAYER B
leads

♣ 2

YOU

At a trump contract with clubs as trump, you win this trick (IF *you don't have any spades to play in your hand*).

It is a rule that you must play a card in the suit your partner leads or the suit the opponents lead. This is known as "following suit". If you can't follow suit, then you can play a trump or discard any other card you want to get rid of.

The word **trump** comes from a fine old Latin word *triumphus*. And a trump card can, indeed, triumph. It automatically ranks higher than any card your opponents put on the table. As you can see from the diagram, the deuce of clubs won the trick from the ace of spades because you didn't have any spades and you did have clubs and the contract was in clubs.

Once you win a trick, incidentally, stack it up neatly in front of you and start the next trick by leading a card. If the opponents win a trick, the person that won it leads.

Now, if you've been reading very carefully, you'll notice we sneaked in a new word on you: **contract**—a very important word because contract bridge is the name of the game we're trying to learn to play.

how "contract" all started

Contract bridge was practically invented by a finely moustachioed gentleman named Harold S. Vanderbilt. Back in 1925 on a long steamship cruise from San Francisco to Havana, Mr. Vanderbilt and three friends decided that the kind of bridge people were playing in those days needed improving. The bidding was wild and woolly. And whether you bid for tricks or not, you got credit for them towards game. Mr. Vanderbilt and friends changed all this.

A bid for tricks became a solemn contract just as if you'd signed your name on a dotted line. And—more important—only the tricks you contracted for counted towards game.

One thing about the old kind of bridge that they kept was bidding for "odd" tricks (the tricks won after the first six tricks). Thus, when you win seven tricks, you have won one "odd" trick. This is very important to remember in bidding. Before you stick your neck out, think how hard it might be to win the first six tricks.

bidding

Bidding is simply a short-cut way to describe how many tricks your hand might win.

The dealer gets the first chance to bid. If his hand looks as if it wouldn't take very many tricks without a lot of help from his partner, he can say "pass" and then the player on his left gets a chance to bid.

With a better hand, he can make a bid. The lowest bid he can make is one club; the highest bid he can make is seven no-trump—which would probably make everybody else at the table keel over in a dead faint.

Once anybody at the table makes a bid, the player to his left may either pass, "double" (which we'll explain later) or make a bid of his own. And here's where the rank of the suits becomes very important.

Any new bid must outrank the last bid. Here's some for-instance bidding to show how this works:

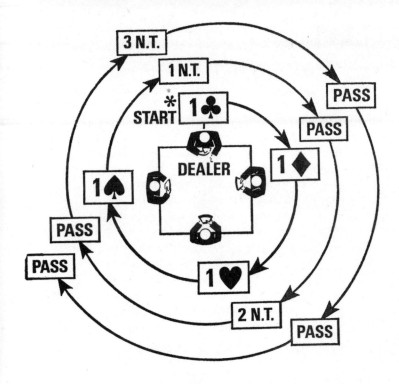

You deal and bid one club (an "opening" bid); next player on your left bids one diamond (an "overcall"); your partner bids one heart; the player to his left bids one spade; and you bid one no-trump, which outranks all the suits.

And here's some more for-instance bidding to show you how to get into the bidding—even though your suit is outranked:

The player on your right bids one spade and your hand is loaded with clubs. If you want to get into the act, you can bid two clubs. When your suit is outranked, all you have to do is bid higher. Thus, if somebody bids three spades or three no-trump, you have to bid four of something to make a legal or "sufficient" bid.

Bidding always goes around clockwise—like the minute hand on a clock. Bidding stops when three people in a row pass. The last bid before the three passes becomes the final contract. Then the play starts.

Let's say *you* made the last bid before everybody passed and your contract is four spades. You become the declarer. The person on your left leads a card, and then your partner must expose all his cards on the table. He becomes the "dummy" and must keep his mouth shut; he can't help you play the hand even though he's your partner.

There *are* a few ways a dummy can legally open his mouth, but it takes a very careful reading of the official rules to find out how. Beginners are generally better off to keep quiet.

One other thing about bidding and about who becomes dummy; the person who *first* bids the suit the contract winds up in or the person who *first* bids no-trump if no-trump is the final contract plays the hand with his partner as dummy.

scoring

(Skim through this section—you learn scoring best through experience).

Mr. Vanderbilt and his friends on the steamship really changed things in this department. They threw the measly game requirements of auction bridge overboard. They set up big bonuses for slams and whopping great penalties for not making a contract doubled. They added the new wrinkle of "vulnerability", which made the bonuses and penalties even bigger.

Practically everything they thought up on that boat trip in 1925 has survived today. Here in a nutshell is the scoring they inspired.

Scoring is done on a sheet of paper with lines printed or drawn like this:

WE
THEY

At the top of the left-hand side of the paper goes the word "We". All the points you and your partner make go on this side of the straight up and down line. On the right-hand side of the line goes the word "They". And all the opponents' points go on this side of the straight up and down line.

The other line—the one that goes across the up and down line—is very important. It separates the "contract" points— the ones you *bid* for—from the points you didn't bid for. Incidentally, you can get lots of points you didn't actually bid for, as you will see shortly. We'll describe these points in detail, but for the time being let's just call them "bonus" points.

Here is another reminder of which points go where:

WE (*if you or your partner are keeping score*)	THEY
Your "bonus" points go up above this line	*Your opponents' "bonus" points go up above this line*
Your "contract" points go here below the line	*Your opponents' "contract" points go here below the line*

Example

WE	THEY
100 (*Honours*) 700 (*Rubber*) 30 (*Overtrick*)	
60 40 ——— 100 ———	

Let's talk about "contract" points first. If your contract is clubs or diamonds, you get 20 points below the line for each trick that you bid for and make. If your contract is hearts or spades, you get 30 points below the line. If your contract is no-trump, you get 40 points below the line for the first trick and 30 points for each additional trick you bid for and make. The tricks you *didn't* bid for and make anyway go above the line in the bonus department. These tricks are called "overtricks".

When you and your partner get 100 points or more *below* the line before your opponents do, you win a "game" and you draw a line under your 100 points or more. You are then "vulnerable" and you start all over again trying to score another 100 points or more below the line. If you succeed, you win a "rubber".

Incidentally, you don't have to make your hundred points all at once. You can bid and make two spades on one hand (60 points below the line); then on a later hand—if the opponents haven't made 100 points in the meantime—you can bid and make one no-trump or two of anything else that adds up to 100 points.

If you win two games before your opponents win a game, you get a bonus score of 700 points.

If your opponents win a game before you make your second game, you only get a 500 point bonus score.

You get more points if your opponents "double" your contract and you make it. Each trick you bid for and make becomes worth twice as much. Thus, one club doubled is worth 40 points instead of 20; one heart doubled is worth 60 instead of 30; no-trump tricks doubled are worth 80 for the first trick and 60 for each trick you bid for and make after that.

If your opponents double and you have an excellent hand and think you can make your contract, you can "redouble".

And then every trick you bid for and make is worth *four* times as much! Thus, a lowly one heart bid doubled and redoubled and made is worth 120 points (game!) below the line.

Now, just in case you're tempted to redouble every doubled contract you bid to get all those juicy points below the line, let's take a look at the points that go *above* the line.

If you're not vulnerable (no 100 points below the line) and you fail to make your contract, the penalty or bonus points that your opponents collect is 50 points for each trick short of your contract. If they double you, they collect 100 points for the first trick you're short or "down" and 200 points for each trick after the first one.

If you're vulnerable (100 points—game—below the line), going down costs you 100 points a trick undoubled and a whopping 200 points for the first trick doubled. Each doubled trick after the first one costs an additional 300 points.

If you're unlucky enough to redouble and go down, you just double the ordinary doubled score.

Other points that go above the line are the ones you get for making more tricks than your contract called for. Your extra tricks don't count towards game, but they're worth 20 each if your contract was clubs or diamonds and 30 points each if your contract was hearts, spades or no-trump.

If you're doubled and make extra tricks, each one counts 100 points not-vulnerable and 200 points vulnerable. If you redouble, each extra trick counts twice as much: 200 not vulnerable; 400 vulnerable. You also get 50 extra points for the "insult" when you make a doubled or redoubled contract.

You get extra bonus points for bidding and making a "slam". A "little slam" (all the tricks but one bid and made) gets you a bonus of 500 points not vulnerable, 750 points vulnerable. A "grand slam" (all the tricks bid and made) gets you 1,000 points not vulnerable, 1,500 points vulnerable.

"Honours" also get you extra points above the line. If one player (even one of your opponents) has four of the highest five cards in your trump suit (like A K J 10), his side gets 100 points. All five of the highest cards in a trump suit (A K Q J 10) in one hand are worth 150 points. All four aces in one hand at a no-trump contract are also worth 150 points.

Remember, a rubber ends as soon as you or your opponents win two games, and the bonus is either 500 or 700 as explained previously.

In case you don't have time to finish a rubber, if one side has a game and the other hasn't, the game is worth 300 points above the line.

Here's a handy guide to scoring that you can refer to if nobody in your game knows how:

CONTRACT BRIDGE SCORING

	Suits			
	♣	♦	♥	♠
TRICK SCORE:				
Each trick over 6	20	20	30	30

NO-TRUMP:	
First trick	40
Each subsequent trick	30

RUBBER BONUS:	
If made in 2 games 700 If made in 3 games	500
If unfinished, winner of one game	300
Part score in unfinished game *(if only one side has part score)*	50

SLAMS *(bid and won)*:

	Not Vulnerable	Vulnerable
Little Slam	500	750
Grand Slam	1,000	1,500

OVERTRICKS:	Not Vulnerable	Vulnerable
Undoubled, each	Trick Value	Trick Value
Doubled, each	100	200
Redoubled, each	200	400
Making Doubled or Redoubled Contract	50	50

BONUS FOR HONOURS IN ONE HAND

Four: 100 points   Five: 150 points
Four Aces at No-trump: 150 points

PENALTIES FOR UNDERTRICKS

	NOT VULNERABLE		VULNERABLE	
	Undoubled	Doubled	Undoubled	Doubled
1 Down	50	100	100	200
2 Down	100	300	200	500
3 Down	150	500	300	800
4 Down	200	700	400	1,100
5 Down	250	900	500	1,400
6 Down	300	1,100	600	1,700
7 Down	350	1,300	700	2,000

If Redoubled,
multiply the doubled values by two.

instant point-count bidding

(Try to memorise this section if possible)

The quickest and easiest way to tell whether or not you have a good hand—a hand that will win tricks—is to use the point-count system. These points have nothing to do with the scoring points you read about in the last section. The point-count system is just a simple way of assigning values to the cards you have in your hand.

Here in a nutshell is how the system works:

HIGH CARD POINTS:

ACE	=	4 *points*
KING	=	3 *points*
QUEEN	=	2 *points*
JACK	=	1 *point*

Add a point for all four aces in your hand; subtract a point if you don't have even one ace in your hand.

DISTRIBUTION POINTS:

A void (*no cards in one suit*)   = 3 *points*

A singleton (*one card in a suit*)   = 2 *points*

A doubleton (*two cards in a suit*) = 1 *point*

The value of high card points is fairly obvious: high cards outrank low cards. Aces and kings usually clobber lesser cards and win more tricks. But lesser cards—even lowly deuces—can have value, too, thanks to distribution.

In a trump contract, if most of the cards in the trump suit are distributed in either your hand or your partner's, this automatically means that one of you will be short in another suit. And the sooner you run out of cards in the suit, the sooner you can start winning tricks with your trump cards. At this point the deuce of trump can be a giant-killer—it can clobber an ace or a king.

Distribution can be important in other ways, too. Very seldom will you have enough aces and kings and queens to make all the tricks you need for your contract whether it's trump or no-trump. You will have to win tricks with "long" cards.

With A K Q J 3 of clubs, for instance, your 3 can take a trick *if* your higher cards can strip the opponents of all their clubs (remember, they *must* play clubs or "follow suit" if they have them). Your club 3 thereby becomes a long card and good as gold.

Here is a typical bid for a suit contract. You add your high card points to your distribution points, and if the total is 12 or more you should start the bidding by making an "opening bid":

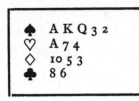

You have 13 high card points plus 1 distribution point for the doubleton in clubs. Open one spade.

To open the bidding with no-trump, you count only your high card points and you need from 16 to 18 of them.

Here is a typical no-trump bid:

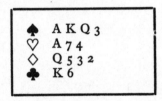

That's a total of 18 high card points (no added points for the doubleton). Open one no-trump.

An opening bid just starts things off nicely. You and your partner need about 26 points between you to make a game in hearts, spades (four odd tricks) or no-trump (three odd tricks).

For a game in clubs or diamonds where you have to bid and make five odd tricks (a total of 11 tricks), you and your partner should have about 29 points between you.

To bid and make a little slam, you usually need 33 points; for a grand slam, 37 points.

Once your partner opens the bidding with a suit, give him credit for at least 12 points and add your honour points to his (in your head, of course). If you have three or four cards in his suit, you can count extra points for distribution as follows:

A VOID	= 5 *points*
A SINGLETON	= 3 *points*
A DOUBLETON	= 1 *point*

As "responder" to his opening bid, if you have three or four cards in his suit give him a "raise" with 5 to 10 points. If he bids one heart, raise his bid to *two* hearts. Then see what happens; it might be all the encouragement he needs to bid more. If he then bids a new suit, he should have more than a minimum of 12 points. On this basis, you should raise or bid something else if you have 9 or 10 points.

If your partner opens one of a suit and you have a hand that *you* would have opened the bidding with yourself, your side probably has game or close to it (his 12 points and your 12 points = 24—only 2 points short of the 26 needed). To show your good hand, give him a double raise (from one spade to three spades) or bid two no-trump or just name a new suit, which forces him to bid one more time anyway.

If your partner opens one no-trump, you know he has between 16 and 18 points. Raise him to two no-trump with 8 or 9 points. Raise him to three no-trump with 10 to 14 points. Raise him to six no-trump with 17 or 18 points. There are other responses to an opening one no-trump bid, but you have enough to remember already.

What if you have a really BIG hand—a "rock-crusher"—and it's your turn to open the bidding? Don't hide your light under a bushel basket; open *two* of something.

For an opening two-bid in a suit, you need a minimum of:

25 points with a 5-card suit
23 points with a 6-card suit
21 points with a 7-card suit

With an absolute bust (less than 4 points) your partner should bid two no-trump to keep the bidding open. With 5 points or more he should keep the bidding open until your side reaches game.

For an opening two-bid in no-trump, you need 22 to 24 points, and your partner can pass with less than 4 points.

If you have 25 to 27 points, you can open three no-trump.

Once your opponents open the bidding, don't abandon hope. You can double at your first chance to bid if you have an opening bid of your own (known as a "take-out" double). This forces your partner to take your double out by naming his longest and strongest suit, bid no-trump or he can pass if he is *certain* that your side can defeat the contract.

You can overcall one or two, depending on whether or not your suit outranks the opponents' suit. Or you can pass and hope either that your partner has something and can make a bid of his own or that your opponents will butcher the play of the hand.

There is, of course, much more to bidding the point-count system than we have given you in the foregoing. The important thing to bear in mind about point-counting is the magic number: 26.

If your points, added to the points you think your partner has, total 26, bid like a lion. If the total is probably less than 26, it's usually safer to bid like a mouse.

If you and your partner have a good chance of having a total of 33 points between you, bid as bravely as a wild bull elephant—you probably have a slam.

don't just sit there . . . bid something!

You've tried to absorb the previous section. Your head is swimming with numbers. Your partner is an experienced player. And PANIC hits you. In this section on bidding and in the next section on play, we'll give you a few pointers that are practically guaranteed panic preventers.

For one thing, if you're afraid you'll forget the number of points you need for a bid, write them down on a piece of paper. Keep this little reminder at your elbow and glance at it from time to time. Nobody will mind, as long as you read it quietly without moving your lips.

Actually, the only numbers that should be indelibly stamped in your mind when figuring out a bid are these:

*** *The entire pack contains 40 high card points.*

*** *26 points between you and your partner will usually produce game.*

*** *33 points between you will usually produce a little slam.*

*** *37 points between you will give you a fighting chance for a grand slam (one of your opponents might hold a king, but he cannot hold an ace).*

Now, here are some easy ways to put these numbers to work:

OPENING BIDS

If you get the first chance to bid and you hold 12 high card points, don't squirm: bid.

Bid one of a 5-card major suit (spades or hearts). If you only have a 4-card major suit, bid one of your minor suits (diamonds or clubs). You can even bid a 3-card minor suit just to start things off. This is known as "opening a short minor"—an exploratory bid that tells your partner that at least you have *something* in your hand.

Actually, you can open with less than 12 high card points if you have a nice long major suit and a few distribution points.

The "rock-crusher" hands that call for an opening *two* bid in a suit or no-trump are easy to determine. Count to 22, and don't forget distribution points if you have a fairly decent suit—major or minor. A suit like A K J 10 x is decent. A suit like A Q J 10 x x is more than decent; you've got a 6-card suit and you're bound to have some distribution points along with it.

PRE-EMPTIVE BIDS

When to make them and what to do about them when your opponents make them.

A pre-emptive bid is legalised highway robbery at the bridge table. Its purpose is to rob the opposition of several chances to bid.

If you are the opening bidder and you are staring at

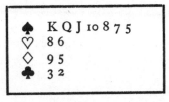

bid three spades!

If the opponents want to bid, they will have to do so at the four level. This takes both courage and cards.

If they double you, the most they can collect is 500 points for setting you three tricks, and if they do the chances are excellent that your bid crowded them out of bidding a game or slam worth as much or much, much more than 500 points.

Now, what should *you* do if your opponents open with a pre-emptive bid?

In this case, the beginner should remember three things:

1. Don't pause for more than ten seconds and then pass. It's unethical because it shows your partner that you had sufficient high cards to pause over.

2. Don't stick your neck out if your bid might cost your side more than 500 points in a penalty double by the opposition. You can generally figure your partner for one trick in making this calculation.

3. When in doubt, double. This is known as a "co-operative double". The bid indicates a shortage of cards in the opponents' suit and reasonably good cards in any suit

your partner might bid in case your own suit is somewhat doubtful. What makes this double "co-operative" is that your partner must co-operate in taking one of two possible courses of action: (1) he can name his best suit, or (2) he can pass your double if he is downright positive the two of you can penalise your opponents severely.

There are other ways to handle pre-emptive bids besides the co-operative double, but this is the safest way for a beginner to handle such bids.

OVERCALLS

An overcall is undoubtedly the most dangerous bid in bridge . . . for the bidder. An innocent 2-club overcall can backfire with such horrendous results as down three doubled, vulnerable—800 golden points down the drain.

Oddly enough, an overcall is the beginner's favourite bid. He will just sit there and pass with a perfectly good opening bid. But once the opponents have bid, he will overcall with absolute rubbish on the theory that he can't possibly get hurt by making such a cheap bargain bid.

One good reason an overcall is anything but a bargain is this: once your opponent has made a bid, his partner has some inkling of the strength of his hand (an opening bid generally indicates three sure tricks). You, the overcaller, stick in your oar, and then your opponent can leisurely put two and two together. His hand, plus his partner's, can often make your overcall a very, very expensive slip of the tongue—for your side.

Beginners—and even experienced players—are much better off reserving the overcall for hands that contain a good, strong, long suit and the likelihood of losing not more than 500 points if doubled. In this case, you can't count on your partner to provide a single trick.

If you don't have a good suit but do have almost an opening bid, make a takeout double. Your partner must respond, and if he has a good suit you'll wind up in a safe contract.

Incidentally, as responder to a takeout double, if you have ten points or more, bid one level higher than necessary. By making this "jump" bid, you alert your partner to the possibility that the two of you might have a game.

RESPONSES

We have already touched on responses in the previous section. Remember we told you to give your partner credit for 12 points if he makes an opening bid of one in a suit. We also told you to add your points in high cards and distribution to his 12 to see if the grand total received adds up to the magic number of 26 (game). Here is an instant guide to the right response, and if it's just too much to memorise add this to the little piece of paper you keep at your elbow.

When your partner opens and you have:

6 to 10 points
and 4 cards in his suit raise his bid to 2.

6 to 10 points
with no support for partner and no good suit of your own bid one no-trump.

6 to 18 points   bid one of a new suit.

10 to 18 points   bid two of a lower ranking suit. (For instance: your partner bids one heart, opponent passes, *you* bid two clubs).

13 to 15 points
and a high card or two in all the unbid suits bid two no-trump.

13 to 16 points
and 3 or 4 *good* cards in his suit raise his bid to 3.

A word of caution goes along with this handy little chart,

however. The lower limits of these responses are based on the assumption that the opponents don't butt into the bidding with an overcall.

If an opponent does butt in, your response becomes what is known as a "free bid". A "free" raise or a "free" bid of a suit of your own had better be based on substantial values in high cards and distribution.

One item that isn't on the chart above is a fairly rare but choice response: a triple raise. This bid describes a hand that is rich in trump support (five cards or more), rich in distribution (a void or a singleton) and *poor* in high cards (less than 9 points). It's a very useful bid. Usually all the opponents can do about it is either sit there and gnash their teeth or make a very dubious double.

REBIDS

When should you bid again as the opening bidder or as the responder? Mental arithmetic to the rescue.

After you have made a response, the opening bidder, guided by the foregoing chart, has a pretty good idea of the upper and lower limits of your hand. A little addition produces two totals—one optimistic and one pessimistic. If the optimistic total (opener's points plus the *most* points you could have as indicated by your response) doesn't approach the magic number of 26, opener should shut up. The only time he can't shut up is when your response was in a new suit. This forces him to rebid. With 12 to 16 points, he can put the damper on your enthusiasm by making a minimum rebid: either one no-trump or two of his suit.

With a good hand of 17 points or more, opener can give you all kinds of encouragement. He can raise your suit, jump in his own suit, bid a new suit or no-trump. Or he can proudly sit up in his chair and bid game.

After you have made one response, should you just rest on your laurels? Not at all.

If you have 11 or 12 points in high cards and distribution, you should respond twice. Your partner may have substantially more than the 12 points you originally gave him credit for. Your second response may be all the encouragement he needs to go to game.

With 13 to 17 points, as responder you should insist on game. Respond the second time by naming a new suit—even a 3-card suit. Your partner is forced to bid again.

When you have 18 points or more, think big. You're in the slam zone. If you don't make a jump response the first time, keep naming new suits and stop short of slam only if partner keeps rebidding his original suit to discourage you.

PENALTY DOUBLES

Most beginners don't double enough. Most experienced players know this and bid accordingly. If you double for penalties when you should, you can reap a golden harvest of bonus points, and thoroughly humiliate the opposition.

Here are a few tips on when to double and when not to.

If partner opened with one of a suit, figure him for about three defensive tricks. Add these tricks to your tricks and if you are reasonably certain you can set the opponents' bid *two* tricks or more, say "double".

If partner opened a no-trump, figure him for four defensive tricks. When he makes a take-out double, figure him for three tricks.

If partner just overcalled or raised your suit, don't count on him for more than one defensive trick.

If partner opened with a pre-emptive bid such as 3 hearts, don't count on him to produce a single trick in his suit on defence. Since he has such a long suit (seven cards or more), chances are the opponents have a void and are just licking their chops in anticipation of your doubling on the basis of his hand. Double on your own hand or just pass meekly.

You'll notice we've been talking about *tricks* instead of *points* when it comes to doubling. High card points are of little value unless your points are in aces. Distribution plays a much more important role in hard-fought competitive bidding. You can have a whole fistful of queens and jacks that can add up to as many as 12 points, and you still can't make a decent double. All the opponents need is a long suit, a shortage or two in the other suits, and they can romp home with their contract. Tricks are what you need to set them. Tricks in their trump suit are the best kind. Just hold K J 10 x of spades and hear a spade overcall on your right after your partner has opened one heart—sheer music to your ears. Your partner probably has at least three defensive tricks for his opening bid of one heart. Unless your righthand opponent is living off rich relatives, he holds A Q 9 8 and a few other spades. Since you are sitting "over" him (on his left), you should win three tricks in his suit. If you have anything in another suit—an ace, a king or a queen—setting him two tricks is almost a certainty. Wait a decent interval, keep the quaver out of your voice when you double, and you and your partner should clean up.

Think about the possibility of trump tricks when you are short in partner's suit. If you have a singleton and he has the ace, you can usually figure on two sure tricks.

Tricks in the suits the opponents didn't bid aren't always guaranteed. Don't count on taking more than two in any particular suit; distribution could rear its ugly head again.

In doubling a no-trump contract, it's best to have a long suit where you are missing only one or two of the top honours and a sure-fire trick on the side that will give you a chance to win the lead in order to cash the established cards in your long suit.

As a general rule, beginners are better off leaving slam contracts *un*doubled. You'll rarely set them more than one, and the risk is too great.

your play

If you aren't positive you know the rank of the cards, the rank of the suits and how tricks are won in trump and no-trump contract, go back and read the first section of this book ("One Card From Another").

You must understand these basic principles very clearly. Once you do, you'll be able to pluck a card out of your hand and plonk it on the table with confidence. Otherwise, you'll just sit there fumbling and annoying the living daylights out of everybody else in the game.

Playing the cards involves either one of two things: (1) offence or (2) defence. On offence, you are trying to make enough tricks to bring home your contract. On defence, you are trying to win enough tricks to "set" or defeat your opponents' contract.

OFFENCE

The Finesse

One of your most useful weapons on offence is the finesse because it's one of the few ways a smaller card can steal a trick from a bigger card. This tricky manoeuvre is best explained by an example:

Your partner as dummy holds ♠ A Q

Your left-hand opponent holds ♠ K 10

You hold ♠ J 9

Your partner's queen is smaller or lower in rank than your opponent's king, but it can steal a trick—quite legitimately, of course. Simply lead to your partner's hand by playing the ♠ 9; then if the left-hand opponent plays the ♠ 10, you play the ♠ Q. Voila, you have successfully *finessed* the ♠ K and won a trick with a smaller card, namely your ♠ Q. The reason you could do this is because it would be sheer folly for your left-hand opponent to play his king; your ace would have clobbered it.

Reverse the cards—you take the dummy's cards and give the right-hand opponent the ♠ K—and the finesse will still work. In short, you can finesse in either direction depending on where you have to lead from.

Incidentally, there are lots of finesses you can try, as you will learn after playing for a while, but bear in mind that only half of them will work. A finesse gives you only a 50-50 chance to win a trick. You should always plan your play to get better odds if you possibly can.

Planning Your Play at a Trump Contract

In bridge, he who hesitates is *not* lost—providing that he hesitates at the right time. The right time is the instant your partner spreads his hand as dummy. Study his hand and then yours. See how they fit. Count the tricks you are most likely to *lose*. Then figure ways to avoid losing these tricks.

All this takes time. If it makes you uncomfortable to delay the game while you go through all these mental gyrations, remember: this is what the experts do. Some of them have been known to stare at dummy's cards or up at the ceiling for as long as twenty minutes before making a play.

It takes time and thought to avoid losers. Here are a few of the ways you can do it:

1. You can take a finesse in trumps or any other suit.

2. You can "drop" a potential loser such as a queen if you and your partner have enough cards and the A K in the suit. Play the A K, and if the queen is a doubleton (Q x) it will drop on your king—a slightly superior play to a finesse when you and your partner hold nine cards in a particular suit.

3. You can ruff (trump) losers. A void, singleton or doubleton in dummy in a particular suit is pure gold if dummy has enough trumps. Strip the dummy of the suit, and then use dummy's trump to ruff your losers.

4. You can discard losers. For instance, if you have A K of a suit in dummy and no cards of that suit in your hand, you can discard two of your hand's losers on the good A K. To make sure you have a "good" A K, you'd better extract the opponents' trumps first. It's always a pity to see a noble king get clobbered by a lonely deuce of trumps. Sometimes, however, you have to take the gamble that your good tricks might be trumped. You try for *quick* discards and hope for the best.

You try for *slow* discards usually by drawing trumps first and then establishing a long suit in dummy. Even though you may have to lose two tricks in your long suit, the discard value of your remaining cards will more than compensate for your temporary loss.

One more decision you'll have to make while you're pausing to plan your play: should you draw out the opponents' trumps right away or not?

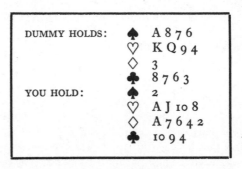

DUMMY HOLDS: ♠ A 8 7 6
♡ K Q 9 4
♢ 3
♣ 8 7 6 3

YOU HOLD: ♠ 2
♡ A J 10 8
♢ A 7 6 4 2
♣ 10 9 4

To count losers here at a four heart contract is futile. If you're forced to play trumps four times to extract them from the opponents, your hand (including your partner's hand) will collapse in a heap of losers. What to do? Your opponents will probably lead clubs, which will ensure your losing the first three tricks. On the fourth trick, however, you take command no matter what the lead is. You cash the ace of diamonds and the ace of spades and then proceed to trump spades in your own hand and diamonds in the dummy, making all eight of your trumps take tricks. Even if one of your opponents holds the remaining five trump cards it will make no difference, because your trumps are all higher. Add your ace of spades and your ace of diamonds to your eight trump tricks and you arrive at a total of 10 tricks or game (six tricks plus four "odd" tricks).

This way of playing a hand, whereby you get the most possible mileage out of your trumps by ruffing back and forth from dummy's hand to yours, is known as "cross-ruffing". It's a possible line of play you should always be on the alert for, especially when it looks as if you have more losers than you can handle.

Planning Your Play at a No-Trump Contract

Planning your play at a no-trump contract isn't too difficult. You don't have to worry about the opponents trumping your good tricks. All you have to worry about is having enough good tricks.

First, count your winners in *high* cards—your aces, kings, queens, etc. If your total doesn't quite come up to the number of tricks you need for your contract, even with a successful finesse or two, look for a suit that can bring you in winners with *long* cards. Maybe you can afford to lose two tricks out of five in a suit. The two tricks you give up might produce three winners in long cards . . . not a bad horse trade. Simply look for a five-card suit in your hand or dummy's, and start losing the tricks you must lose right away.

A word of caution about no-trump, however: no-trump contracts are about one trick harder to play than trump contracts, so don't bid no-trump willy-nilly. You might regret not having a few trumps to take care of the opponents' high cards.

DEFENCE

Your Opening Lead

A staggering number of contracts are won or lost on the opening lead. Finding the right opening lead is a combination of science, art and intuition. There are a few guiding principles that you would do well to familiarise yourself with. Most of the time they produce better results than intuition—even female intuition.

1. **Lead your partner's suit.** If you have three worthless cards in it, lead the highest (6 5 3). If you have a doubleton honour, lead the honour (Q 6). If you have three cards or more but no honour in his suit, lead your lowest card.

2. **Lead your own suit.** If you have a sequence of touching honours such as Q J 10, lead the top of the sequence, the queen. If you have A K, lead the king and once it wins the trick your partner will know you also might have the ace. If you have an A K doubleton, play the ace and then the king—an "echo" that informs your partner that you only have two cards in the suit and that you might be able to trump the third lead of the suit.

3. **Lead an unbid suit.** Sometimes when the opponents fail to mention a particular suit in their bidding, it can indicate a serious shortage of strength therein. If your partner has any top cards at all, he is most likely to have them in this suit. Lead "top of nothing" (9 7 2) or "top of sequence" (J 10 9).

4. **Lead through dummy's suit.** He might have a "broken" suit such as A Q 10 9. If your partner has the missing pieces, the king and the jack, he may be able to make at least one of them good.

5. **Lead a trump.** You may bust up a beautiful cross-ruff or cut down the ruffing power of the dummy. When dummy has bid two or three suits, he is bound to have a shortage in the unbid suits. Often this is your cue to plonk down a trump or—if you have the ace and a little trump—play trumps twice.

6. **Lead a singleton or a doubleton.** This is a particularly good lead if you have a short but potent trump holding such as K 9 2 and your partner has shown some signs of life during the bidding. He may have an ace or a king to gain quick "entry" into the play . . . whereupon he can return to the suit your singleton was in, and you can make one of your little trumps good by ruffing.

7. **Lead a long suit and "pump the chump".** If you have a good collection of trump cards (four or more), it's usually a good idea to lead a suit you think the declarer may have

to ruff. If you keep leading this unit at every opportunity, you may wind up with more trumps than the declarer—and this is an embarrassing and costly predicament for him.

8. **Lead your longest and strongest suit.** Defending against a no-trump contract, your idea is to win as many long card tricks as you can in addition to your high card tricks. With this in mind, it almost always pays to open the fourth highest card in your longest and strongest suit (K 10 9 6 2). This starts you on your way to establishing long card tricks. If you and your partner have enough entries, eventually your deuce can win a trick.

The only time you *don't* lead "fourth best" are: (1) when you have a long sequence of touching honours (A K Q J 3) or (2) when you have what's called an internal sequence (K J 10 8 3). You lead the jack in hopes of knocking out one of the opponents' high cards in a hurry.

Some General Principles of Defence

The first thing you must do on defence is figure out exactly how many tricks you need to set the contract. If the opponents have bid four of something, that means they have only contracted for 10 tricks. You'll have to win three tricks ("book" for the defence) before you can even start setting them.

Total up your rock-solid certain tricks, your highly probable tricks, and then plan your defence just as carefully as you would plan the play of one of your own contracts. Plan before you make your opening lead. Plan after dummy exposes his hand. Plan as the play progresses and you gather more evidence concerning what your partner and the declarer hold.

Defence is the toughest part of bridge. It calls for more calculation, more alertness than any other phase of the game. And you have poor yardsticks to go by. Here are a few of them, but remember: each must be tempered with common sense and even ignored at times—vigilance and experience will tell you when.

1. **Second hand low.** When you are second to play to a trick, it rarely pays to squander your high cards by clobbering little cards with them. Play a waiting game. Maybe your partner can take the trick more cheaply· In a finesse situation, maybe your opponent might chicken out and not take the finesse. High cards are best used to overtake other high cards. Don't waste them on deuces and threes unless you have an urgent reason to take a trick. An urgent reason might be to get in fast in order to return partner's first-led suit if you suspect he led a singleton and can now ruff.

2. **Third hand high.** When you are third to play to a trick, play as high as you need to take the trick or force out a high card in the fourth hand. This doesn't mean you automatically play your highest card. Sometimes your next highest card will do the job you want it to as in this case.

YOU (*third hand*) HOLD:

K J 3

DUMMY HOLDS: FOURTH HAND HOLDS:

Q 6 5   A 7 4

PARTNER HOLDS:

10 9 8 2

Partner leads the deuce, dummy plays low, you should play the *jack*—not the king. The jack will smoke out fourth hand's ace quite nicely; your king will be good as gold and in perfect position to capture the queen next time your partner leads.

3. **Play through strength.** When the dummy is on your left, it usually pays to lead through a strong but slightly

"fractured" suit, such as A Q 10 or K J 9—especially if the suit isn't too long. Otherwise, you may be doing the opponents' work for them and setting up long card tricks for discards.

4. **Play up to weakness.** "When the dummy's on your right, lead the weakest suit in sight." And that's a sage old motto. It enables your partner to hoard his strength in the suit until after the declarer plays. Then he can decide whether to pounce or sit back quietly—a rare freedom of choice.

5. **Return your partner's suit.** When your partner has made the opening lead, give him credit for having led the suit he did. He may have had a singleton or doubleton. He may have had an honour that he led away from or "underled". Unless you're in a great rush to carry out some fiendish plan of your own, it's generally a good idea to return a card in his suit.

6. **Signal high-low.** When you want to encourage your partner to lead a suit for the third time, discard first a high card in the suit and then a low card. This tells partner that you either have only two cards in the suit and you can ruff the third round, or it tells him that you have a missing top honour in the suit.

Remember these general principles on offence and defence are not graven on tablets of stone, but some direction is better than none. Use these principles when you have nothing better to use, and your game will at least be adequate—for a beginner it will be astonishingly good.

good luck and keep calm

This little book has given you the irreducible minimum of knowledge about the bidding and play of contract bridge.

Now it's up to you to get your feet wet.

Your first few sessions at the bridge table might give you mild jitters. You may stumble over things that experienced players take for granted and in stride.

This is all perfectly natural, normal and to be expected. You are a beginner. Don't be ashamed of it.

Even the beetle-browed experts who glare at you over their cards were beginners once. Don't let them bully you. Charm them with your innocent eagerness to share their knowledge. After a hand is over, ask them how *they* would have bid it or played it. You'll learn something and you'll also pull their fangs.

Your worst jitters will come from occasional agonies of indecision. If you sit there stewing too long, you will get yourself and your opponents into bad feeling. It's much better to make the wrong bid of play after a reasonable pause.

You can then apologise sweetly to your partner after he bites your head off as he explains why your bid or play was wrong. Again you'll learn something.

Almost everybody loves a beginner. Your presence makes them feel smug and superior. The only really unpopular beginner is the one who makes the same mistakes over and over again.

Keep track of your "goofs"—either in your head or on a slip of paper. Then *do* something about them. Re-read the section in this book that concerns itself with the areas in which you erred or embark on a more stringent programme of self-improvement.

This book is a cram course to enable a beginner to sit down at the bridge table with as few qualms as possible. Here are a few suggestions for a more extensive course:

Read the "free" bridge lessons in your daily newspaper. For the price of a daily paper, you can get a bridge lesson from famous bridge experts.

Play as often as you can. Experience is *not* the best teacher in bridge, but it helps. Experience in actual play helps you determine what areas are weakest in your game. Firming these up involves reading a good book, taking bridge lessons or asking questions. Play often, but don't expect rapid improvement by *just* playing.

Be a "kibitzer". The word comes from a German word for a bird. To be a proper kibitzer, you must be a songless bird. Look over the players' shoulders, run around the table flapping your wings—but let not a single "peep" issue from your lips. Keeping your eyes and ears open can be enormously instructive. Keep your mouth shut is the better part of valour. Talkative kibitzers have been known to have had their heads bitten off . . . at the ankles.

On this ominous note, I wish you all the luck—and the aces—in the world.

the language of bridge

(or How To Sound Like An Expert)

Auction: an old-fashioned version of bridge; nowadays it means the bidding. A review of the auction simply means: "Who bid what?"

Balance: a bid to re-open the bidding when your opponents' bidding shows weakness. You can often balance after two passes with as few as 10 high card points.

Balanced Hand: a hand wherein the suits are fairly evenly distributed, such as 4-3-3-3. An unbalanced hand is one with a long suit and a singleton or doubleton.

Bid: an educated guess as to how much your hand is worth on offence and defence. You can bid—depending on your cards and your courage—any number of spades, hearts, diamonds, clubs or no-trump. If your hand is worthless, you can pass. If you think your opponents are in deep water with their bid, you can double. They can redouble, also. Some doubles have a special meaning (see below). Some bids have an unusual meaning (see Convention).

Blackwood: a sudden bid of four no-trump which requests your partner to indicate the number of aces in his hand by responding as follows: with no aces or all four, 5 clubs; with one ace, 5 diamonds; with two aces, 5 hearts; with three aces, 5 spades. Kings are indicated the same way after partner bids five no-trump.

Blank: no cards (a void) in a suit.

Book: book on offence means the first six tricks you must win before you can start making your contract; on defence, it means the number of tricks your opponents must win before they can start defeating your contract.

Business Double: a double for penalties. See the section on scoring for just how many points you collect if you defeat your opponent's contract double. The penalties can be staggering.

Cashing: a synonym for taking a trick. You either cash tricks or lose them.

Contract: the partnership that bids the highest *contracts* for a specific number of odd tricks (tricks won after the partnership wins the first six tricks). Their final bid becomes the contract.

Convention: any bid that has a special or unusual meaning agreed to by a partnership. Blackwood is an example because four no-trump indicates a request for aces— a special meaning—rather than a desire to play the contract at four no-trump.

Co-operative Double: a double of a pre-emptive bid that requests your partner to co-operate by either passing or naming his best suit—whichever bid he thinks will be most profitable.

Cover: playing a higher ranking card than one your opponents have led. You cover a queen with a king, for instance.

Cross-ruff: trumping different suits back and forth from your hand to your partner's. When you are "caught" in a cross-ruff, the opponents do it to you.

Cue Bid: a surprise bid of one of the opponents' suits or a surprise bid of a new suit after the trump suit has been agreed upon. It usually indicates an ace or a void in the suit bid.

Declarer: the player who winds up playing the contract with his partner as dummy.

Deuce: the two card of a suit—lowest card in the pack.

Discard: when you discard, you play a card (usually worthless) other than trump or the suit led.

Distribution points: the points you add to your high-card points in estimating the value of your hand. Length or shortness in suits gets you points.

Double: a two-edged sword. It can be an attempt to penalise your opponents (business double) or it can be an invitation to your partner to bid (co-operative double, take out double).

Doubleton: two cards in a suit.

Down: going down means failing to make your contract.

Draw: leading a suit often enough to extract the opponents' cards in that suit. You *draw* the opponents' trumps. This is also known as "pulling" trumps.

Drop: you drop an opponent's king, for example, if you play your ace and the poor wretch had a singleton king. Sometimes it takes two or three leads of a suit to drop an opponent's high card.

Duck: a foxy move whereby you pass up your first opportunity to take a trick. You duck sometimes to enable your partner to run off the entire suit when you take your trick later and lead a low card in suit that your partner can over take or cover.

Dummy: the hand that is exposed on the table once the contract has been established.

Duplicate: a form of tournament bridge whereby the cards are kept as dealt in slotted boards and played again by other players. This way you can compare scores on any given hand. The partners that average the highest scores are the winners.

End Play: giving one of your opponents a trick at a time when he will be forced to make a lead that benefits you.

Entry: a trump or a high card that provides transportation from your hand to your partner's or vice versa.

Finesse: a way a smaller card can sneak past a larger card and win a trick. You finesse a king by leading toward an ace-queen combination. If the king is on your left and your opponent doesn't play it, your queen can win the trick—the simplest form of a finesse.

Fishbein: a convention that comes in handy when the opponents try to bamboozle you out of the auction by making an opening bid of three or four with a long suit and very few high card points. With Fishbein you bid the next higher ranking suit over clubs, diamonds or hearts. This says, "Partner, I have a good hand, so name your best suit or bid no-trump if you can stop the opponents' suit." Over an opening 3 spade bid, Fishbein calls for a 4 club bid if you want your partner to show his stuff.

Follow Suit: playing a card in the same suit led by you or the opponents—a *must* if you or dummy have one.

Forcing Bid: a bid that forces your partner to respond unless he wants his head bitten off. A "cue" bid whereby you bid the same suit your opponents have bid is forcing upon your partner. Many conventional bids force a response. If you open 2 clubs, for instance, your partner must respond even with absolute rubbish in his hand . . . in which case he bids two diamonds to put a damper on your enthusiasm.

Game: one hundred points or more scored below the line. See scoring section.

High Cards: usually aces, kings, queens and jacks, but sometimes a three can be a high card if it captures an opponent's deuce.

Honour: an ace, king, queen, jack or ten. With four honours in a suit you have "100 honours" and score one hundred points above the line. Five honours in a suit gets you 150 points above the line. The only catch is that the final contract *must* be in the suit with the honours for you to get credit for these bonus points.

Jump: any response or overcall that is at least one level higher than need be. Most jump responses force the opener to bid again. A jump overcall nowadays is just a nuisance bid made with a long suit to deprive the opponents of opportunities to bid.

Lead: the play of the first card on a trick. The player to the left of the bidder puts down the first card after the bidding is over, making what is called the *opening lead*.

Major Suits: hearts and spades.

Minor Suits: clubs and diamonds.

Newspaper Hand: a hand that is tricky enough to rate comment by your favourite newspaper's bridge columnist. Following is a typical one:

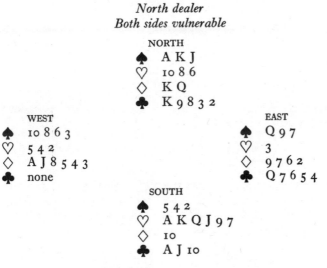

North dealer
Both sides vulnerable

NORTH
♠ A K J
♡ 10 8 6
♢ K Q
♣ K 9 8 3 2

WEST
♠ 10 8 6 3
♡ 5 4 2
♢ A J 8 5 4 3
♣ none

EAST
♠ Q 9 7
♡ 3
♢ 9 7 6 2
♣ Q 7 6 5 4

SOUTH
♠ 5 4 2
♡ A K Q J 9 7
♢ 10
♣ A J 10

NORTH: 1 N.T.   EAST: pass   SOUTH: 6♡   All pass
Opening lead: ♢ — A

The tricky part of this hand is discarding a club at the second trick after the dummy's diamond king wins the second diamond lead. After drawing trumps, South leads the ace of clubs. Then he leads the jack of clubs and overtakes it with dummy's king. He then leads the nine of clubs. If East covers with a queen, South trumps, gets back to dummy with a high spade and discards his losing spade on the now good eight of clubs. If East ducks the nine of clubs, South pitches his losing spade instantly.

Notice how the different players and their hands are

labelled "North, South, East and West"—A nautical navigational note reminiscent of Mr. Vanderbilt's famous steamship cruise where contract bridge got its start.

No-trump: a contract wherein only the highest cards can win tricks.

Odd Tricks: tricks won after the first six tricks won by the side who gained the final contract.

Open: the first bid by anybody at the table.

Overcall: a bid over (higher in rank than) an opponent's bid.

Overtrick: any trick in excess of the ones you bargained or contracted for.

Part Score: any score less than 100 points (game) bid and made in one deal. In rubber bridge, part scores are extremely important. Two of them can easily add up to game.

Pass: usually a pessimistic bid to warn your partner that your hand isn't worth shouting about. A "trap" pass is just the opposite. You have a good hand, but you hope to trap the opponents into a foolhardy bid by pretending that you have a weak hand.

Penalty: the cost of failure to make your contract. Penalties are scored above the line and don't count toward making game.

Pips: early playing cards were often decorated with pictures of fruit such as "pippins" (apples). This became shortened to pips and now stands for the present-day symbols on cards.

Point Count: a way of evaluating your hand. Honours and distribution get you points as explained earlier.

Pre-emptive Bids: these bids (also called "shut-out" bids) involve bidding as high as you can as fast as you can with a hand that's long in one suit but not very strong in high cards. Chances are that you'll be set, but chances are equally good that your opponents have game and won't be able to find it because you have crowded them out of several chances to bid at a low level. You may sacrifice 200 or 300 points, but it's much better than letting them make 600 or 800 points (game and rubber).

Psychic Bid: a phony bid indicating either strength or length that you don't have. It can confuse the daylights out of your opponents. It can also backfire and confuse your partner.

Quick Tricks: almost guaranteed tricks that you can win with aces and kings. . . *if* the opponents don't trump them.

Raise: bidding to a higher level in a suit your partner named first. A "free" raise is made over an intervening bid by one of your opponents and usually shows good support for partner's suit.

Redouble: a way of indicating to your partner that your opponents have made a bad double and that you have either a good hand or a good chance at making your contract.

Revoke: the unpardonable crime of not following suit when you could have. Usually penalised by two tricks that you have to hand back to your opponents.

Rubber: the first partnership to score two games wins the rubber, thus making extra points.

Ruff: ruff means to trump.

Sacrifice: a semi-suicidal bid whereby you contract for more tricks than you can possibly make. A sacrifice bid generally pays off if the penalty points collected by the opponents add up to less than they could have made playing and making their own contract.

Set: same as defeat. You set the opponents when you defeat their contract.

Short Club: a convenience—not a convention. You bid a short club (or diamond in some cases) when you don't have a long, strong major suit and you still have a hand with enough points for a bid. Your minimum number of cards in your short suit is three and it usually pays to have an honour in it.

Singleton: one card in a suit.

Slam: a contract for twelve (small slam) or all thirteen tricks (grand slam).

Squeeze Play: an advanced play whereby you give one or both of your opponents an impossible choice of discards.

Stayman: a conventional bid made in response to an opening no-trump bid. In its simplest version, responder bids 2 clubs which requests the opening no-trump bidder to name his 4 card major suit if he has one. If he doesn't, opener bids 2 diamonds and it's up to responder to determine where the contract is to be played.

Strip: to exhaust a hand of a particular suit by leading it repeatedly.

Suits: spades, hearts, diamonds, clubs.

Table: "on the table, partner" means you must next play a card from the dummy's hand which is lying there on the table.

Takeout: a bid by your partner other than a raise.

Takeout Double: a double of the opponent's bid—usually at your first opportunity to bid. Also known as an "informative" double, because it informs your partner that you have a decent hand and that you'd like to hear from him.

Tenace: the best and the third-best cards in a suit in one hand such as A Q.

Trump: *a trump* is a card in the suit named in the final contract; *to trump* means playing a card in this suit if you can't follow suit.

Undertricks: the number of tricks that fall short of your contract when you're set.

Void: no cards in a particular suit. Same as a blank.

Vulnerable: once your side has won a game you are vulnerable—vulnerable to higher penalties for reckless bidding.

Whist: an ancient form of bridge played during the 17th century in noisy English coffee houses. Whist meant "shut up" an expression used so frequently during play that it became the name of the game.

Yarborough: a hand with no card higher than a nine. Named after Lord Yarborough who offered 1,000 to 1 odds before dealing that the taker would *not* be dealt such a miserable hand. The actual odds against such a hand are much higher, so the wily old gentleman made a tidy sum from this bet.

a little private practice

(Do-it-yourself exercises on just a few of the basic things you need to know to be a good player)

POINT COUNTING

How many points are these hands worth if you have the chance to open the bidding?

1. ♠ A K J ♡ Q J 10 ◇ A Q 9 ♣ J 10 9 8
2. ♠ Q J ♡ K J 2 ◇ 3 2 ♣ A J 7 6 5 4
3. ♠ A K 10 9 8 7 ♡ Q J ◇ Q 3 ♣ 9 8 6
4. ♠ A K Q 10 9 8 7 ♡ 2 ◇ 3 2 ♣ J 10 9
5. ♠ K J 9 6 ♡ Q 8 7 ◇ K J ♣ A 7 6 2
6. ♠ A K 10 ♡ A Q 9 ◇ J 10 9 ♣ K Q 10 9
7. ♠ A Q 10 9 8 ♡ Q J 10 ◇ A K 10 9 ♣ A

Answers

1. Eighteen "good" points in high cards—the upper limit of an opening one no-trump bid. How can points be anything but "good"? See the answer to the next hand.

2. Twelve points in high cards plus 1 point in distribution (1 point for the diamond doubleton) for a total of 13 "poor" points. If your opponents hold the ace and king of spades, your Q J will be worthless. If your left-hand opponent holds the K Q 10 of clubs, you will take only one trick in the suit. Your points are poor because they don't represent rock-solid tricks. Don't panic—bid one club not vulnerable, but don't expect miracles unless your partner responds with enthusiasm.

3. You have only 12 points in high cards, but this hand illustrates two important items about bidding for beginners. The first is that even though many bridge books tell you to pass most 12-point hands, a beginner will get his head bitten off by a seasoned partner if he underbids. As my grandmother once put it, "Open light and overcall strong, and you'll make friends of your partners."

   It is much better if you get your feet wet with a light or even skimpy opening bid than to sit there and hide even a faint light under a bushel basket. Besides, the light is much brighter on this hand than you might think.

   The second item this hand illustrates is the need for assigning point-count values to long suits. In this case you have a six-card spade suit—good length—and it's worth one point for the fifth spade and one point for the sixth spade. Anything else assigned to this length would be highly inflationary, but it does bring the total value of the hand up to a healthy 14 points, which you *must* open. Remember this: long cards are worth points, too (one point each for the fifth, sixth, etc.).

   There is one other item this hand illustrates: the sheer folly of assigning too much point count to doubleton (or singleton) honours. You'll notice that in hand No. 2 the only doubleton we counted as a distributional point was the diamond doubleton. The spade doubleton was counted on the basis of high cards only. Remember this, too: short cards should be counted only in terms of their high-card value. Don't count them twice as high-card points *and* distributional points. This will get you into trouble almost every time.

4. You have only 10 points in high cards, but your long cards in spades are worth 3 additional points. You can probably win seven tricks in spades with no help whatsoever from your partner. In other words, you lack only three tricks to make game. Open one spade and hope your partner responds with a bid other than "pass".

5. Again a hand loaded with potentially poor points. The total in high cards and distribution is 15, but the hand is worth much less than that if there is vigorous bidding on your left such as an overcall of one no-trump. If there is vigorous bidding on your *right*, however, your hand is worth more than 15 points. Your kings are sitting nicely over the aces and should win tricks. Position even more than points often determines the true value of a hand.

6. You have 19 high-card points—too much for an opening bid of one no-trump (16 to 18 points), but not enough for an opening two-bid (22 points). Open one club, and if your partner responds with a bid of one in any suit, rebid two no-trump (one level higher than necessary). This indicates a hand that was too good for an opening one no-trump bid.

   If he bids one no-trump, showing six points or more, raise him to three no-trump.

   If he bids two clubs, rebid three no-trump and keep your fingers crossed. You *should* make it—if he has something in diamonds.

7. Twenty high-card points—not enough for an opening two bid, but potential money in the bank. Open one spade, and regardless of what your partner responds, rebid one level higher than necessary in diamonds (a jump rebid). If your partner can respond in anything, you may have a slam. Game is certain.

OVERCALLS AND TAKEOUT DOUBLES

The opponent on your right has just made a pre-emptive bid of three hearts. What do you bid with each of these hands?

1. ♠ A K Q J 10 2   ♡ 4 3 2   ◇ 7   ♣ Q J 10
2. ♠ A K J 10   ♡ 2   ◇ Q J 10 9   ♣ A K 7 2
3. ♠ K J 9 8 6 ♡ J 4   ◇ K J 9   ♣ K J 3

The opponent on your right bids one spade; what do you bid with each of these hands?

4. ♠ A J 10   ♡ Q J 10 9 8 7   ◇ K 3 2   ♣ 2
5. ♠ 2   ♡ A K 10 8   ◇ K J 10 9   ♣ K Q 8 2
6. ♠ 4 3 2   ♡ K J 8 7 2   ◇ K Q 8 7   ♣ K

Answers

1. Bid three spades even if you are vulnerable. The most you are likely to go down is three tricks, and you have 150 honours in your suit to cushion the shock.

2. Make a co-operative double. If your partner has a long suit and few hearts, he will name his suit and you will be able to support it with vim. If your partner has a fistful of hearts, he will pass and your double will return a handsome profit.

3. Pass. With a weak bid on your right, if the opponents have any strength, it is most likely to be sitting on your left. In which event your kings and jacks would be clobbered by aces and queens.

4. Bid the hearts. Even though you are missing the ace and king of your suit, the rest of the suit is money in the bank. If your partner bids diamonds, bid game in hearts.

5. Double. This is a takeout double and says: "Partner, I am woefully short in spades, but I have an opening bid of my own. Please show me your stuff."

6. Discretion is the better part of valour with this rubbish. Pass. If you bid two hearts with such a poorly textured suit, your left-hand opponent could fatten up on your penalty points if he happens to hold both length and strength in hearts.

RESPONSES

Your partner made an opening bid of one heart. What do you respond with each of these hands?

1. ♠ A K Q 6 5   ♡ 4 3 2   ♢ 5 4 3 2   ♣ 10
2. ♠ 5 4 3   ♡ 4 3 2   ♢ A K J 10 9   ♣ A 5
3. ♠ A 8   ♡ 5 4 3 2   ♢ K 10 9   ♣ Q J 10 8
4. ♠ 9 8   ♡ Q J 8 6   ♢ K Q 9   ♣ K Q 10 9
5. ♠ Q J 7   ♡ 8 6   ♢ A Q 10 8   ♣ 10 9 8 6
6. ♠ 7   ♡ 10 9 7 6 4   ♢ A K 9 8   ♣ 10 9 8
7. ♠ A K Q   ♡ 10 9 8   ♢ A K J 10 9   ♣ Q 10

Answers

1. Bid one spade. This is more informative than just raising his suit. Besides, your heart support is nothing to brag about.

2. Bid two diamonds. Your hand is strong enough to raise the level of the bidding.

3. Raise your partner. Bid two hearts to give him some mild encouragement.

4. Give your partner a *double* raise. Bid three hearts—one level higher than you have to bid. This shows him good trump support and 13 to 16 points.

5. Bid one no-trump. You have 9 high card points—more than enough to make sure your partner gets another chance to bid.

6. Give your partner a *triple* raise. Bid four hearts—two levels higher than you have to bid. With your singleton, your trump support and your good diamonds, you should have an excellent go at game. If you get set, be comforted in the almost certain knowledge that your opponents missed a game in spades or clubs.

7. Think big. You have 19 high card points which should put your partnership into the slam zone. Tell him the good news by jumping in a new suit (a jump "shift"). Bid three diamonds—one level higher than necessary.

NO-TRUMP CONTRACTS

1. North (dummy): ♠ K 3
   ♡ Q 8 6
   ◇ A Q 9 3 2
   ♣ 5 4 3

   South (you): ♠ A 6 5
   ♡ A K 5
   ◇ J 10 8 5
   ♣ A Q 6

You are the declarer at three no-trump. Your left-hand opponent makes the opening lead of the spade queen. How do you play the hand?

2. North (dummy): ♠ A 3
♥ Q J 10 9 8 7
♦ 5 4 3
♣ K 2

South (you): ♠ K 5 4 2
♥ 3 2
♦ A K Q
♣ A 5 4 3

You are declarer at three no-trump, and your left-hand opponent leads the diamond jack. How do you play the hand?

Answers

1. You have seven sure tricks in top cards. You must find two more to make your contract. The diamond suit will provide these tricks even if your right-hand opponent holds the diamond king, but you might as well try the finesse anyway. Win the first trick in your hand and lay down the diamond jack. If your left-hand opponent has the king and hoards it, play a small diamond from dummy and lay down the diamond 10 for another finesse. If the finesse loses and your right-hand opponent returns a club, climb right up with the ace and cash your good diamonds for four no-trump.

2. You are in luck. Your opponents didn't lead clubs or spades, the suits in which you have only two stoppers. This gives you what the experts call "timing" on the hand. You have the time to develop your long suit (hearts) before the opponents can develop their tricks in the black suits (spades and clubs). Because they led diamonds, you have a chance to drive out the ace and king of hearts. This you must do immediately. No matter what they return after winning these tricks, you can stop it. The two top hearts are all you need to lose. You'll make five no-trump.

1. North (dummy): ♠ 10 9 2
                  ♡ 2
                  ◇ K J 7 6 5
                  ♣ K 4 3 2

   South (you):   ♠ A K Q J 8
                  ♡ A 4
                  ◇ A 4 2
                  ♣ A 6 5

You are declarer at five spades. The opening lead is the heart king. When you survey your hand and the dummy, you see immediately that you have a loser in clubs and a possible loser in diamonds. How do you play the hand to be sure of making your contract?

2. North (dummy): ♠ K Q 6 5
                  ♡ A 5 4
                  ◇ 6 5
                  ♣ A Q J 10

   South (you):   ♠ A J 10 9 8
                  ♡ 3 2
                  ◇ K Q 9 8 7
                  ♣ 7

East-West are vulnerable.

The bidding:

North	East	South	West
1♣	1♡	1♠	Pass
2♡ (!)	Pass	3◇	Pass
4♠	Pass	4 NT	Pass
5♡	Pass	6♠	Pass
Pass	Pass	Pass	

Opening lead: Queen of hearts.

Problem: How do you avoid losing a heart?

Answers

1. The key to this hand is to delay drawing trumps until you have used one of dummy's trumps to take care of your heart loser. Plonk down the ace of hearts. Then lead the four of hearts and trump it in dummy. Then—and only then—can you afford to draw trumps. If the finesse of the diamond jack works, you will make a small slam. If it fails, you make your contract anyway.

2. You make this hand by listening to the bidding and by a tricky manoeuvre known as a "ruffing finesse".

   The bidding illustrates several items you should note carefully:

   North opens one club—not one spade—to make it easier for his partner to respond (he can bid *one* of anything) and to make it easier to make a rebid (if his partner responds one of anything except no-trump, opener can then show his spades at the one level).

   East overcalls one heart. He has a six-card suit and all the nerve in the world.

   South makes a "free" response of one spade—his best *major* suit (with nothing but rubbish he would have been free to pass).

   North gets so interested in the hand's game potential that he "cue-bids" hearts. This indicates either an ace or a void in hearts and commits the partnership to arrive at a game bid.

   South now shows his diamond suit.

   North now shows his powerful spade support.

   South knows a good thing when he hears one and bids four no-trump (Blackwood) asking his partner how many aces he has.

North bids five hearts—indicating two aces—a conventional bid that *doesn't* indicate any real interest in playing the hand in hearts.

South has heard enough. He crosses his fingers and bids six spades.

Losing a trick to the ace of diamonds is a certainty. The problem is to avoid losing a heart, too.

If you have listened to the bidding carefully, you can find a place to park your heart loser.

Remember East (your right-hand opponent) overcalled your partner's opening one-club bid with a bid of one heart. Unless he has a producing oil well in his backyard, you can safely assume that he had something besides hearts for his overcall.

You can assume that if you took a normal finesse in clubs (leading a low card from your hand and playing the 10 in dummy), it would lose a trick to his king. Back would come a top heart, and you'd be down two!

So you take a ruffing finesse. All in good time, however.

First, you take the opening trick and the ace of hearts in dummy. Then, you extract the opponents' trumps. Lead spades twice, playing the ace and the jack. Lead your low club and play the ace of clubs in the dummy.

Play the ten of clubs. If your right-hand opponent plays low, ditch your heart loser.

If he climbs up with his king of clubs, ruff it (trump it). Then you can lead back to dummy and park your heart loser on the queen or jack of clubs.

Either way, you can make your right-hand opponent miserable. A very nice feeling—for you.

DOUBLED CONTRACTS

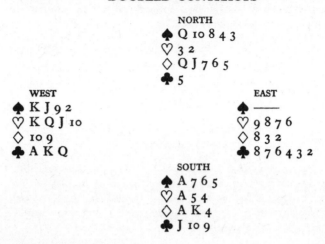

NORTH
♠ Q 10 8 4 3
♡ 3 2
◇ Q J 7 6 5
♣ 5

WEST
♠ K J 9 2
♡ K Q J 10
◇ 10 9
♣ A K Q

EAST
♠ —
♡ 9 8 7 6
◇ 8 3 2
♣ 8 7 6 4 3 2

SOUTH
♠ A 7 6 5
♡ A 5 4
◇ A K 4
♣ J 10 9

1. You are at a contract of four spades and your left-hand opponent (West) made a resounding double. His opening lead is the king of hearts. How do you make the hand?

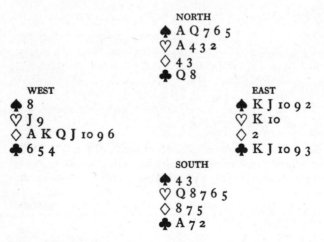

NORTH
♠ A Q 7 6 5
♡ A 4 3 2
◇ 4 3
♣ Q 8

WEST
♠ 8
♡ J 9
◇ A K Q J 10 9 6
♣ 6 5 4

EAST
♠ K J 10 9 2
♡ K 10
◇ 2
♣ K J 10 9 3

SOUTH
♠ 4 3
♡ Q 8 7 6 5
◇ 8 7 5
♣ A 7 2

2. West opens with a pre-emptive bid of three diamonds. Your partner—bless his feeble mind—bids a co-operative double. East passes. You (South) are forced to co-operate by bidding three hearts. West passes. Your partner comes to his senses and passes. East, who has been lying in the grass, says "DOUBLE!" The opening lead is the spade eight. How do you avoid a complete disaster?

Answers

1. Take the heart king with the ace. You have work to do, so delaying does you no good. This leaves you with a heart loser and a club loser. The problem is to avoid losing two trump tricks in spades. There are four trump cards outstanding in the opponents' possession. How they are split is a matter of conjecture, but since West doubled, you may reasonably assume that he has most if not all of the trump cards. Lay down your ace of spades, and you will see right away that you can finesse all of West's trumps except the king.

Lead a low spade toward dummy's hand. West will undoubtedly go right up with his king because he wants the lead. He will lead his good queen of hearts and come back with his ace of clubs. He has taken his book, three tricks, but now he must surrender the lead no matter what he does. You can trump either a heart or a club lead in dummy.

Lead a small diamond in dummy to the ace of diamonds. Lead a low spade from your own hand and cover any spade he plays as cheaply as possible. (If he plays the nine, you cover with the ten, not the queen). Return to your hand with a low diamond to the king. Another spade lead accounts for all the trump cards, and you can now take your three good diamond tricks in dummy—making your contract, *doubled*!

2. You are going to lose two diamonds, a club and possibly two hearts. You have a 50-50 chance to avoid losing a spade by taking a finesse, but therein lies disaster. If you play the queen of spades from dummy, East will cover it with his king and lead his singleton diamond. West will win with his ace and return a diamond—boom—East will trump in order to return a spade. You will be caught up in a racking cross-ruff and your opponent will cash *four* tricks in your trump suit. Add these losers to your losing spade finesse, the two diamond tricks, and your club losers, and you wind up being set four tricks doubled.

Now let's see what happens if you start with the assumption that you're faced with a hopeless situation and you plan your play to go down gracefully and economically.

First off, you must climb right up with the ace of spades on the opening lead. West has announced with his preemptive bid that he has a long suit so he must be short in another suit. East doubled, so there is every likelihood that he holds the power—in this case, the king of spades.

Your next move should be to bang down the ace of hearts and then lead a little heart. This way your opponents will win only *one* trump trick. Add this to your other losers and you are set only *one* trick instead of four. The difference in penalty points is staggering (600 points—not vulnerable; 900 points—vulnerable).

*　*　*　*　*

These have been just a few samples of the fun you can have playing the fascinating game of bridge. And the more you practise and read, the more fascinating the game becomes. Once again I would like to reccommend that you read the daily free bridge lessons in your newspaper. They let you practise in private with the guidance of the top bridge experts. In no time at all, you'll sharpen your game to a razor's edge.

index